Five Things You Can Do in 30 Minutes to Improve Your Riding Forever

By

Michael Schaffer

This page deliberately left blank

Copyright ©2012 Michael Schaffer
Po Box 421
Riegelsville, Pa. 18077

Photos ©2012 Michael Schaffer

Cover Drawing By Susan Harris
(www.anatomyinmotion.com)

Disclaimer

ISBN-13: 978-1483992426
ISBN-10: 148399242X

Kindle Edition
ASIN: B00AO7E4X8

Acknowledgements

Thanks to Katie Wright, who appears in the pictures, Lois Tashjian who allowed herself to be roped into editing this, and to Susan Harris for the drawing of me on the cover and in figure 11. I've enjoyed having it on my wall for many years, now I share it with you.

Contents

This page deliberately left blank

Introduction

Riding correctly is a matter of learning to ride in confidence and comfort.

The suggestions in this article are the corrections you can use to make yourself and your horse more confident and comfortable. These are the corrections I make with most new students in the first few minutes of their first lesson. They are the easiest corrections to make in all of riding.

In fact these corrections are so easy and so obvious I'm surprised I have to make them so often, yet there are a lot of students riding in incorrect positions with their horses in unsuitable frames at unrealistic energy levels. The result is they and their horses are miserable when they shouldn't be.

The really good news is, figuring out what is right for you and your horse is simple, easy, and quick because, as you're about to see, it's just common sense.

This page deliberately left blank

First - Get on the level

In order to ride comfortably you need a well balanced saddle. A saddle is well balanced if it fits the horse and provides you with a level place to sit. The most common saddle fit error is a saddle that goes uphill – the seat is up in front and lower in the back. The actual seat – the place where you're supposed to sit – should be level or very slightly sloping down toward the front. If the saddle is uphill, or you're not sure if it's uphill, try putting a folded towel or riser pad under the back of it. A word of caution here, this will only work on a saddle that fits your horse reasonably well to begin with.

While it's possible that a riser pad will be sufficient as a permanent fix, it's also likely a qualified saddle fitter will be required. Ok - that will take more than 30 minutes, but a folded towel or riser pad under the back will show you in just a few minutes how much better riding on a correctly balanced saddle can be.

Figure 1: This saddle looks pretty good, but it's going up hill and puts the rider too far to the rear.

Figure 2: With a folded towel under the back of the saddle it is much more level. You can use this or a riser pad to feel how much of a difference it makes.

This page deliberately left blank

Second - Sit like you stand

When you stand, you don't keep your heels down - you keep them under you! So, that's the way you should ride.

Although you've probably been told a few thousand times to have your "heels down", that only works well if you have the elasticity of a 12 year old or are a professional who rides 5 or 6 horses a day. For most adult amateurs trying to keep their heels down forces their feet forward which throws them out of balance.

To feel correct balance and how it's affected by forcing your heels down, stand up (right now!) with your feet about shoulder distance apart while allowing your arms to just hang naturally. Bend your knees slightly and "settle down" a little until you find a comfortable steady position. Now, if you look down, you'll notice your heels are directly under your hips which are right under your shoulders. Also notice that you're not falling forward or back, but are in perfect balance and are comfortable standing just that way. Let's call this your "balance position."

While standing in your balance position notice that your heels are level with, and have about as much weight in them as the balls of your feet. Put more weight in your heels as though pushing down on them (lifting the balls of your feet does the same thing) and you'll feel how that creates an imbalance which tends to make you fall back.

If you stand in your balance position again and then put more weight in the front of your foot, you'll probably notice this causes you to lean more forward. What is true for you standing on the ground is true while sitting on your horse. Too much weight in your heels makes you fall back. If you have too much weight in your toes, you'll tend to fall forward.

If your stirrups were adjusted too short to force your heels down, you will always be falling back. Conversely, if your stirrups are too long and you're pushing down in your toes to reach them, you'll tip forward.

The bottom line is, if you adjust your stirrups and position your feet so that you have the same balance in the saddle as you did in your balance position while standing on the ground - that is the perfect position -- and stirrup length for you.

Figure 3: Standing in the balance position, shoulders, hips and ankles are in line and perpendicular to the ground.

Figure 4: Most riders push their feet forward and rock their upper body back when they try to force their heels down.

Figure 5: Conversely, if stirrups are too long and riders have to stand on their toes to reach them, it tends to pitch them forward

Figure 6: Here the riders heels are up just a bit, but they are under her hips and she is balanced.

Figure 7: In this photo her heels are down but her feet are in front of her and she is falling back.

Third - Keep Your Elbows Bent

One of the absolute worst and most common errors in equitation today is riding with straight arms. I can't even say people do this because it's theoretically correct since it isn't. Riding with straight arms creates all kinds of problems for horse and rider. It pulls the riders shoulders and entire upper body forward and out of balance. It creates tension in the rider which prevents him from feeling the horse. Also, it breaks the connection between rein and seat.

The connection between rein and seat is what gives the rider the ability to mold the horse with his aids as he uses hands, seat and legs in a deliberate and coordinated way. Without this connection and coordination the hands tell the horse one thing, the seat may say something else entirely, and the riders legs flail away stride after stride to not much purpose at all. I know you've seen this – now you know what causes it.

You can feel correct connection and how it helps to coordinate your aids with another simple ground exercise. Begin by standing in your balance position with your arms hanging down. Notice your elbows are directly under your shoulders and just above your hips. (Figure 8)

Now leave your elbows at your hips as you bend them and bring your hands together at roughly the height of your belly button. (Figure 9) Notice how doing this actually improves your already good balance as it helps you to bring your shoulders back, open your chest, sit up straighter while simultaneously sinking deeper into your seat and knees. It does exactly this in the saddle too – it helps you to sit up straighter and deeper in the saddle with a longer leg. Pretty easy eh? Because it is easy, you can sit on a moving horse this way and remain relaxed. Being relaxed lets you feel your horse and your horse feel you.

While still standing like this, notice that anything you do with your seat (wiggle it a little) affects your hands, and any move you make with your hand affects your seat. That's connection. It is only when your hands, seat and legs are connected like this that you can use them in a deliberate and coordinated way to give your horse single coordinated aids. Your seat won't actually move when you're sitting in the saddle, but your horse will feel the slight changes in pressure of your seat and legs through the saddle.

Now, just straighten your arms and notice that all those wonderful qualities you had an instant ago disappear completely! (Figure 10) Your shoulders and chest which were back and open are now rounded and collapsed. Instead of feeling as though you're sitting slightly back and deep in the saddle, you feel and actually are being pulled forward and out of the saddle.

With your elbows bent and near your hips, there was a connection between rein and seat – not now. Now you can wiggle your butt quite a bit without affecting your stiff hand much. Try it.

I said your hand was stiff now because it has to be – holding your arms out in that position puts a fair amount of strain on your shoulders – and that's just standing there on the ground for a few moments! Trying to ride a horse in this position is a terrible strain. There is no way to do it correctly so riders end up getting stiff and against their horse, which makes the horses stiffen and brace against the rider. This is made worse because you can't "give" to your horse if your elbows are already straight. All you can do is rotate your arm up and down from your shoulder. That's no way to ride.

I could go on but I think I've made the point – bend your elbows.

Figure 8: Standing in the balance position your elbows hang directly below your shoulders.

Figure 9: Allow your upper arms to
hang and bend your elbows. When you
do this while sitting in a saddle you'll sit
deeper and more correctly.

Figure 10: Pushing your hands forward
and down with straight elbows pulls
your shoulders and upper body forward
and out of balance.

A hallmark of the functional, comfortable, and balanced seat is that you can use your aids in a deliberate and coordinated way. Part of this is the concept of the rein aids working with or "going through" the seat, and the seat working with or going through the reins.

Figure 11: Many years ago Susan Harris, the author and artist, did this wonderful drawing of me warming up a horse at a show. At that time I had very little gut and plenty of hair -- a situation that has reversed somewhat dramatically. What hasn't changed and never will, is the need to keep your elbows bent, so there is a straight line from bit to elbow and the rein goes through the seat. This drawing captures a moment in which this principle is exemplified.

Fourth - Go like you walk

Of all the crazy things humans have thought up, the idea of squeezing a horse with your legs to make him go has got to be near the top of the list. Yes, you can teach a horse that he should go when you squeeze, but we also teach horses to go when we cluck our tongue, touch him with a driving whip, or look at him a certain way in the round pen. Of these methods, the least practical and most contradictory technique is squeezing with our legs.

The method of tightening our legs is contradictory because it's tough to do without also tightening our seat and back. All three of these things actually make it more difficult for the horse to move freely forward. This is why many riders use the technique of bracing the back and tightening the seat to tell horses to stop.

Squeezing with our legs is also silly because it's hard to do and there is nothing about squeezing that "makes a horse go." Most green horses don't "go" when they feel legs squeeze them - they scrunch up and stop, back up, or buck. It is only after they have learned that they are supposed to "go" when we squeeze that they do go.

Since we have to teach a horse what our "go" signal or aid is, we might as well pick one that is easy to do and fulfills my definition of what an aid should be: something we do with our hands, seat, and legs that requests, encourages, and allows the horse to do what we want. I find riding the way we walk is the best method for doing just that and the easiest for horse and rider to learn.

What's that? "Ride the way we walk." What does that mean?

Most of us react this way because we don't really know how we walk - we just walk. We certainly don't pay any attention to how we "begin" to walk. It turns out, we have two ways we almost always use when we begin to walk and both are totally analogous to the way horses begin to walk.

One typical way we begin to walk is by leaning forward from the ankles until we begin to fall forward. Then we stick a foot out to prevent a total collapse, and then the next foot and then the first again. That's it, we've begun to walk by falling forward just as a horse does by falling on his forehand. These three pictures show a human beginning to walk by falling forward.

Figure 12 A,B,C: We begin to walk by leaning forward from the ankles until we begin to fall forward, then we stick a foot out, then the next foot, then the first again.

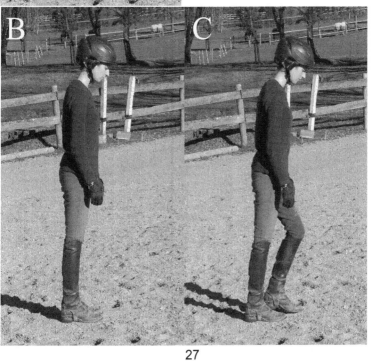

Figure 13 A,B,C: Another way we begin walking is by pushing our hips forward.

This method is really useful when asking a horse to "go" because it asks the horse to go in a way that requests, encourages, and allows him to do so. Using it is simplicity itself - when sitting on a standing horse, just sit up a little as you push your belly button forward.

Since most horses haven't been taught that this is a "go" message, they will likely ignore it at first. So, when introducing this, you'll have to give it meaning by immediately following up with a message your horse does understand – this could be a cluck of the tongue, touch of the whip, saying "giddy up", or taking one rein and leading him around in a circle just enough to get him moving his feet a little. If you find you need to use your legs, take them off the horse a little and let them fall gently back to him instead of squeezing.

Once he's going for a few steps, have him stop, relax for a moment, and then ask him to go again. Of course, to do this we have to have a correct way to ask him to stop.

This page deliberately left blank

Fifth - Stop Like You Stop

The way you stop yourself when walking is surprisingly similar to the way you begin to walk when standing. As you're walking along, just make yourself a little taller and let your hips come forward a bit. Try it now a few times — just stand up, push your hips a little forward to start walking, and then make yourself a hair taller as your hips come forward to stop walking.

Even though you're sitting when riding, it should feel the same — the only addition is what to do with your hands. To go, allow your hands to move with your belly button as you push it forward a little.

To stop just raise your hands a little as you sit up. Just raising your hands, even a small amount, has enough influence on your seat to create a sufficient seat aid. If you had contact before asking for the stop, keep the same contact or even soften it a bit, as you raise your hands. At this stage don't be concerned with your horse stopping immediately — we're just teaching him the concept of stopping when you ask him this new way, so give him some time to figure it out.

As your horse does begin to stop allow him to stretch over his topline so he can step under with his hind legs. If your horse thinks your softening the rein means he should keep going, ask again, softening as he begins to stop once more. If after two or three repetitions your horse hasn't stopped, you may have to just stop the horse as if to say -"Hey! When I do this it means you should stop!"

Of course you can't work on stop without also working on go. So just get on a circle, not too big, not too small, and ask your horse to go, then stop, go, then stop, go then stop, go, stop, go, stop...

As you repeat this don't try to fix other things. Ask him to go enough that you're moving and then ask for the stop again. Don't waste time going round and round. The more times you can go and stop in a minute, the fewer minutes it will take the horse to understand how you're asking for them.

Doing it this way it shouldn't be long until it's as easy and takes about as much thought to go and stop while sitting on your horse as it does while standing on the ground. Once you have that, you can begin the rest of his training.

...

This page deliberately left blank

Other Works

From

Mike Schaffer

www.mikeschaffer.com

Riding in the Moment -
Discover the Hidden Language of Dressage

This book shows that all the figures and movements are based on five "first tier basics" — Go, Stop, Turn In, Move Out, and Soften. We build from these to create all of the qualities we want in our horses. Mike also shows that in training we need to use aids than we do with finished horses. Using these ideas he explains how to take a horse to mid-level dressage (roughly Prix St. Geo.) in a way that makes sense to horse and rider.

This book is available in Kindle format on Amazon:

It's also available in soft cover at his website and Amazon.com

This page deliberately left blank

Right From the Start
Create a Sane, Soft, Well-Balanced Horse

Mike Schaffer's Right from the Start shares his knowledge of
the fundamentals, as well as his unique way of starting horses,
whether they are young and untrained, or older, and needing a
new reschooling regimen. With work from the ground, as well
as lessons on the horse, he reveals his training process. Using
understandable aids, he teaches the horse to soften and move
into the rider's hand. And, by controlling the horse's direction
and angle, he teaches him to bend, control his speed, and
balance his movement. Eventually, the end becomes the
means, and what the horse has learned blends seamlessly into
specific riding disciplines such as dressage, jumping,
eventing, endurance, trail, and just plain riding for fun.

This book is available in Kindle format on Amazon:

It's also available in **soft cover** at his website and on Amazon

Printed in Great Britain
by Amazon.co.uk, Ltd.,
Marston Gate.